I dedicate this book to my dear grandchildren, Jillian, Daniel, Lauren, and Aaron. During the war, between battles, they were always on my mind as they are now in my heart.

BREAKING MY SILENCE

Marvin Sussman

U.S. Army VII Corps
4th Cavalry Reconnaissance Squadron A Troop

Seventy-five years after the D-Day landings, Marvin Sussman, age 95, who fought from the beaches of Normandy across France to the Hurtgen Forest and the Bulge, recounts experiences of what was demanded of soldiers who together must face death every day in combat: the actions, the brotherhood and the sacrifice.

ISBN: 9781096645207

Designed by Sally Freedman

Printed in USA

Acknowledgements

I have quite a few family and friends to thank for their persistence in pushing me first to share and then to write down my war stories.

First, there is my beautiful, talented, intelligent granddaughter, Lauren Sussman, who nags with undeniable charm and made me put oral history into words on record. There is also her mother Marie, who insisted that I tell my story with other veterans at an American Legion event, where the MC was Scott Whitehair, a genius who runs the live storytelling community in Chicago and its environs. He persuaded me to participate in an evening of storytelling at Mrs. Murphy and Sons Irish Bistro on Chicago's Lincoln Avenue. A standing ovation there led to more stories at that venue and another in suburban Lake Forest's community hall, where a check for $200 gave me professional standing. (I now have mail from *Billboard,* just like any other "pro"!)

I must also acknowledge the zeal of my niece, Gail Sussman-Miller, encouraged by her husband Steve. She recorded most of these events and created a YouTube channel for them, where you can also see my speeches in high school auditoriums. And I thank my sons, Mathieu and Marc, and their wives, Marie and Mary, who organized two evenings of a one-man show at Chicago's Filament Theater on Milwaukee Avenue. Proceeds were donated to the National Veteran's Art Museum, and a video recording was professionally produced.

Thanks also to my son Michel and his wife Sandy, for their long-distance encouragement and appreciation; my dear sister-in-law, Alyce Heman, for convincing me I had something important to contribute; my niece Sandy and her husband Ron for their non-stop support; and Sally Freedman, for being excited enough by these stories to put them into the form of a real book, which is now in your hands.

And I thank the Park Place of Elmhurst Christian community, my home during this adventure, for the freedom of mind it provides for its retired family of 200 or so – an atmosphere so important to a writer. May this volume spur other "PP" residents to tell their own stories. Everyone has stories to tell!

Finally, I must mention the encouragement I always had from my beautiful, dear and recently-departed wife Miguelle, who knew good writing when she read it and still thought I was a good writer.

As you see, I needed and got a lot of encouragement.

Prologue

THE FIRST STORYTELLER we know about was Homer, and his first story was the Iliad, *a war story. So war stories go back to the beginning of literature. Everyone wants to hear a war story, but war veterans don't like to tell war stories. Why stir up unpleasant memories?*

And even if a veteran wanted to tell a war story, how is it even possible? Who can really describe the horror of war? Certainly not the vast majority of veterans. I have been reading all my life, but writing is another matter. So, why am I telling these stories?

Since my war experience, I have watched other Americans go to war, several wars, none of which were defensive wars, and all of which were controversial, to say the least. I believe that few politicians understand much about either armed force or diplomacy. In their ignorance, they find it safer to use the armed force than to expose their own incompetence at diplomacy.

By the public's assent or by its silence, soldiers are much too easily sent overseas to kill and to die. I wrote these stories to explain to the public what combat demands from the soldier, hoping that the public's knowledge will somehow make it more difficult for our leaders to send soldiers overseas to kill and to die.

Addressing York High School, Chicago, 2018

Norm and me

My father Simon (l), Aunt Alice, brother Norman, me and mother Esther; my older sister Eleanor was the photographer.

Growing Up

I was born in 1923 into a world much different than today. We lived in Lawndale, in the center of Chicago, six miles west of the lake. One of the earliest of my memories, before kindergarten, is that of sitting under a blanket on a sled with a wooden railing around the sides and being pulled by my father along a path through a canyon of snow that was much higher than my head.

I walked two blocks to kindergarten, crossing Roosevelt Road with my sister, 18 months older than me. I remember that it was a very large room with about 50 children. There was singing and dancing and storytelling, but no reading or writing. My sister brought her school books home. I read along with her, so that I learned to read before entering first grade.

I was seven years old when the economic depression began in 1930. My Aunt Alice and my Uncle Milton moved in and lived with us in our rented apartment to save expense. They had no children. In the morning, my mother was always busy with my baby brother and my sister. I remember my aunt waking me up on school-day mornings with a glass of orange juice in her hand. She wore a hat, ready to go to work as a saleswoman in a Loop department store. At that time, women always wore hats.

The orange juice was needed to cover the awful taste of a spoonful of oil taken from the liver of a codfish. The oil contained vitamin D, and doctors believed that it could help prevent tuberculosis. TB is a lung disease now usually cured by antibiotics, which did not exist then. At that time, recovery from TB was very difficult, if at all possible.

It is probably true that the cod liver oil was not very useful in preventing tuberculosis. But I still believe it is also possible that I am here only because every school-day morning, I was awakened by an angel with a hat instead of wings, and was saved by her love potion. It is certainly true that all of us are here only because we were loved. In effect, I had two mothers! When I think that now there are so many children being raised by a single parent or by foster parents or even no parents, I understand why there are so many troubled children – and adults, too. We were fortunate children to have so much care.

I had almost all of the childhood diseases: measles, chicken pox, mumps and scarlet fever. At that time, there were no vaccines for those diseases. Each time, I had to stay home for weeks. That's when I started to do a lot of reading in my father's book collection. He had 3,000 books, some on philosophy.

When I was 10 years old, I had to help my parents by delivering 60 newspapers before 6:00 a.m. every morning for $10 a month. I had to wake up at 4:30 a.m. From my bicycle on the sidewalk, I had to throw a rolled-up paper onto a front porch out of the rain or snow. If I missed, I had to wipe it dry. That was my first job.

Almost all of the families on our block were either Italian or Jewish. Our parents spoke their native language in their homes, and we could understand our parent's language but we always answered in English. That's why we could not speak our parents' language very well. We also learned a lot of the language of our friends' parents. Of course, we mostly heard and spoke English when outdoors. I also studied Latin and German in high school. All of these languages later became valuable.

Most of my friends were Italian. Attilo was my best friend. Sometimes we did homework together in his home and I ate delicious Italian food. His favorite baseball player was Joe DiMaggio, an all-star Yankee center-fielder. My favorite player was Hank Greenberg, an all-star Tiger home-run hitter. We argued a lot about baseball and other sports. Attilo had four brothers and two sisters. Attilo's oldest brother spent some time in the Joliet prison because of dealing in liquor during the prohibition of alcohol drinks.

When I was 12 years old, baseball became the most important thing in my life. That year the Chicago Cubs won the 1935 National League championship, and all of my friends and I and the entire city went absolutely wild! Then the Cubs lost four games in a row to the Detroit Tigers in the World Series, and our disappointment was crushing. I never again could be really attached to any professional sport team. Children should be careful when they give their heart away! Young hearts can be so easily broken.

I jogged one mile to John Marshall High School in the morning and back for lunch. Then I did the same thing in the afternoon.

In ROTC at John Marshall High School

In every schoolroom, there were six rows of seats and eight seats in a row. Usually, all the seats were filled, but I don't remember the teachers having much trouble keeping order in the class. That was because we were all children of immigrants and knew that school was the most important thing in our lives.

Attilo and I enlisted in 1942 and went our separate ways for training. I spent the winter of 1942-43 in the Black Hills of South Dakota and the spring and summer of 1943 in the Mohave Desert in California. Then we were given a two-week furlough to go home and see our family and friends. Attilo was in the Army, but had been sent to study at the University of Chicago for special training. We were able to spend a weekend together. Both of us were now older and no longer boys.

Attilo was assigned to the infantry, and in November 1944, on Leyte Island in the Philippine Archipelago, he was killed by a Japanese sniper. He was not even 21 years old.

After the war I went to visit his family. There were two blue stars and one gold star in the window. Attilo's brother, Clay, had also been wounded. We all did a lot of crying. I found out that I could still understand Italian

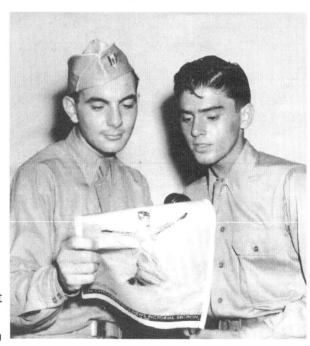

With Attilo

and even speak it when I had to say something important.

Two years after the war ended, Attilo's body was brought home, and all his friends and neighbors attended his funeral. I was one of six veterans who were pall-bearers. There was a military burial service at the Queen of Heaven Cemetery in Hillside. A squad of soldiers fired a rifle salute and a bugler played "Taps." It was a cloudy day, but as the coffin was lowered, the sun broke through the clouds. When that happened, Attilo's oldest sister, Domenica, whispered to me that Attilo had entered heaven. An army officer gave his mother a flag. Going away, I heard her mutter bitterly: *"Una bandiera non mi dara nipotini!"* which means "A flag won't give me grandchildren!"

I remember thinking that, when we were children, I should have admitted to Attilo that Joe DiMaggio really was a more valuable baseball player than Hank Greenberg. The things that children argue about are never as important as they think they are. Treasure your friends!

AND SO IT BEGINS ...

IN PREPARATION FOR THE INVASION of Normandy, the 4th MCG was assigned the task of capturing the Iles Saint-Marcouf, 6,000 yards out from Utah Beach, in order to neutralize the formidable fortifications the Wehrmacht had erected there. Along with this mission, the 4th was also to land two troops ashore in order to link up with elements of the 82nd Airborne Division and the 101st Airborne Division behind German lines to give the paratroopers armored support.

At 0430 on 6 June 1944, elements of A Troop 4th Squadron and B Troop 24th Squadron landed on the Saint-Marcouf islands. Cpl. Harvey S. Olsen and Pvt. Thomas C. Killeran of Troop A (4th) and Sgt. John S. Zanders and Cpl. Melvin F. Kinzie of Troop B (24th) swam ashore armed only with knives, to mark the beaches for the landing craft. They became the first seaborne American soldiers to land in France on D-Day. When the invasion began, the troops rapidly captured the islands with no resistance; the Germans had evacuated, but 19 men were wounded or killed due to enemy mines. On 7 June, just south of Utah Beach, a platoon of Troop B 4th Squadron linked up with elements of the 82nd Airborne and managed to ambush a German convoy in a mechanized cavalry charge, causing the enemy to retreat and leave behind 200 casualties. Rough seas prevented C Troop from landing, but they linked up with elements of the 101st on 8 June.

WAR STORY 1: THAT DAMNED GCT!

THE THING IS, German soldiers were permitted to surrender only when they ran out of ammunition and, on that July day in Normandy, they were trapped and wanted to surrender and were getting rid of their ammunition by dumping it on us: burp guns, machine guns, mortars, 88s. We, the dumped-upon, Troop A of the 4th Cavalry Reconnaissance Squadron, were crouching in foxholes dug into hedgerows, pasture walls of solid earth a meter thick and two meters high with trees growing out of them. We were answering their fire by calling down an artillery barrage on their hedgerows. A light drizzle was Mother Nature's pox on both our houses.

The date was D+37, July 13, 1944. From Utah Beach, the VII Army Corps had cut across the peninsula, trapping German troops against the sea. Cut off from supplies, the "Krauts" were running on empty stomachs and would get their next meal in a prisoner of war camp.

And the sooner they ran out of ammo, the better for us! Since D-Day, A Troop had lost seven dead and 22 wounded out of 140 men at full strength. But, advancing toward the end of the peninsula, our mood was good. With the war going our way, we could think seriously about going home.

If you are wondering why cavalry troopers were crouching in foxholes, so was I. I enlisted in the cavalry to avoid being drafted into the infantry. Nobody told me that when the cavalry dismounts, it becomes infantry!

Of course, we teenagers knew nothing about the service. Pearl Harbor was attacked less than six months after my high school graduation. During 1942, I had to choose a branch of service or else be drafted during 1943. So, as autumn leaves were falling, I raised my right hand and took a step forward into the cavalry, which was just then trading its horses for jeeps and armored cars.

I won't bore you with induction details but, to follow this story, you have to know something about the GCT, the General Classification Test. The GCT was an aptitude test given to everyone at induction. The test was non-verbal. We were asked to look at drawings and reason about them under a time constraint.

For example, we had to count the number of cubes arranged in various shapes. For drawings of right-hand and left-hand threaded screws shown in all possible orientations, we had to show their direction of motion when twisted either way. There were analogies to be recognized, etc. So, the GCT score, one number, allowed an officer to judge one's ability to observe carefully and to reason well and quickly.

Long before my enlistment, I was attracted by an ad in *Popular Mechanics* magazine that was offering to sell the GCT test. I mailed a few bucks for the sample problems, and over some six months I did some serious cramming. Then, at the downtown Chicago induction center, I aced the GCT!

Of course, we were not given the test results, but a few months later, on a cool winter morning in California's Mohave Desert, I was approached by A Troop's clerk, Corporal "Red" Johnson from Minnesota, who began this dialog.

"Sussman, do you know that you have the highest GCT in the squadron?" (A squadron has three line troops and a HQ troop, over 500 men.)

"What's a GCT?" (I was playing it cool.)

"That test you took at the induction center. Your score was 184."

"What was normal?" (Still cool.)

"Normal is 100. The next highest score was 134; a lieutenant in C Troop."

"Red, what was your score?" (The troop clerk was picked for being sharp. The troop clerk ran the troop. He had to see that everyone got what they needed!)

"I got 112."

"Very interesting."

Interesting, but forgotten during five months of desert heat followed by a year of training in east Texas, crossing the Atlantic, training in southern England, D-Day, and a month of combat. Forgotten by me, but not forgotten by army records.

On that rainy July day in Normandy, while I was dozing off in my foxhole, a call was passed down the hedgerow, "Sussman, go see the sergeant!" A clod of dirt in my face woke me up. (Yes, if you go without sleep long enough, you can fall asleep while mortars are dropping nearby!) I grabbed my rifle and, with rain poncho and helmet, I ducked to the end of the hedgerow.

Sitting in his corner foxhole, Sgt. McDermond had a mean look. "Sussman, what did you do? The captain wants to see you!"

"I didn't do nothing!" (The double negative was obligatory.)

Ducking my way past two hedgerows to the rear, I heard my name and, looking around, I saw Capt. Benge in a deep foxhole.

"Sussman, get down here! Mortars are coming in!"

It seemed fairly quiet back there, but I quickly joined him.

"Sussman, what did you do? The colonel wants to see you!"

"I have no idea, SIR!" with a salute and no double negative.

"Well, Corporal Buck has a jeep to take you to Squadron. Look sharp!"

Another salute and I double-timed to the roadway. During a three-minute wet and bumpy ride through quiet fields, Isaac Buck, from South Dakota, asked me what this was about. I had no idea. And that was the truth.

Col. Dunn's tent had a folding card table with a light bulb hung over it and a telephone and some papers on it and a small file drawer next to it. There was more, but my eyes were fixed on the colonel, seated on a folding chair at the table. He was a West Pointer, short, trim and wry. He had a low but commanding voice and a confident look that always impressed us.

He returned my salute with an "At ease, trooper!" and then asked the following questions:

"Your name is Marvin Sussman?"
"Yes, SIR!"

"Your rank is private?"
"Yes, SIR!"

"You are a rifleman?"
"Yes, SIR!"

"You serve in a line platoon?"
"Yes, SIR!"

"You have been in combat over 30 days?"
"Yes, SIR!"

"You are over 18?"
"Yes, SIR!"

"You are under 21?"
"Yes, SIR!"

"You have a high school diploma?"
"Yes, SIR!"

Then, a minute of silence while he examined some papers. Then he said: "Trooper, you are the only man in the squadron who qualifies."

"Sir?" I was puzzled.

"Trooper, you are going to West Point for four years. They will make you an officer and a gentleman. You will leave immediately. Corporal Buck will get your duffel bag. Sign this."

All of that was said in a gravelly monotone, like reading a grocery list, while handing me a typed sheet of paper.

I was probably standing there with my mouth open, stunned, motionless.

My mind was racing.

That damned GCT!

Four years and then an army career!
Out of a foxhole into hell!
This damn war was almost over!
The Krauts were giving up!
The Red Army was near Warsaw!
With our capture of Saipan, our air force could destroy Japan!
If I could stick this thing out for a few months, I could be home free!
And Col. Dunn wants my signature!
Now!

Moreover, I had enlisted for combat service because I wanted to accept a risk that I could not ask others to take for me. Now, Col. Dunn was taking away that risk.

Choosing a branch of service was the most important moral decision of my entire life and probably of the lives of every volunteer. I had chosen to face danger rather than relative safety.

During most of 1942, it appeared that we could very likely lose the war, in which case most of us would be dead or would wish that we were dead. Under those circumstances, we were choosing the amount of danger that we dared to face. All my friends were making their choices: Air Force? Infantry? Marines? Nobody was mentioning Coast Guard or Quartermaster, except as a joke.

Was that male bravado? Yes, there was some of that but there was also a real need, if we survived, to be able to look in the mirror without shame, every morning, for the rest of our lives. So, going to West Point for four years, avoiding the risks, leaving it to others, did not seem right.

And how could I sit in a classroom, listening to a lecture, while A-troopers were lying in foxholes, listening to incoming death and destruction? How could I concentrate on facts, numbers and words while remembering faces, names and wounds?

A-troopers were not just friends. During more than 20 months, eating almost 2,000 meals together, we became close companions. And a month of combat had turned companions into brothers. I was closer to a couple of those guys than I was to my own brother, five years younger than me. Leaving them for West Point did not seem right.

Col. Dunn must have sensed my hesitation, because he explained further: "The 7th Army Corps has a quota of five men with combat experience to be sent to West Point. And by God, one of them is coming out of my squadron!"

(An army corps has about 2,000 squadrons. Out of 400 squadrons, only one would send a cadet to West Point.)

"Yes, SIR!"

That was the only possible response to a commanding voice that was no longer low. Col. Dunn's Irish eyes were not smiling. No matter how I got that high GCT score, I was at least intelligent enough not to argue with a colonel with his mind made up. To read and sign the paper, I reached under my rain poncho into my shirt for my eyeglasses and fumbled them.

"You wear glasses, trooper?"
"Yes, SIR!"

"Trooper, you may return to your unit."
"Yes, SIR!" (With gusto!)

Followed by a sharp salute, a snappy about-face and a hasty retreat.

Today, West Point will take you with your eyeglasses, false teeth and hearing aids, if not with artificial limbs and a pacemaker. But that was 1944.

So, back to the foxhole and the 88s! I explained the trip to squadron HQ as a need to straighten out some records. The truth would have only brought on a ribbing, well-deserved and never-ending. I could have saved a few dollars, a lot of time spent cramming for the GCT, and all that day's turmoil.

The thing is, I now have another counterfactual to mull over: What if I had not reached for my glasses? All I had to do was sign the damn thing! Probably, on arrival, West Point would have accepted me with good-enough eyes. How would that alter my life? I would probably get to play poker with future famous generals! I could become a famous general! Or I could be killed leading an infantry platoon in Korea! Et cetera.

But that's all fantasy. The reality is that, on that rainy July day, during that three-minute wet and bumpy ride through quiet fields with Isaac Buck, going back to the foxhole and the 88s, I did feel relieved, if not happy. But a few months later, soaking my butt in the Hurtgen Forest or freezing it in the Bulge, there were moments – oh yes, there were moments! – when I really missed being at West Point on the Hudson.

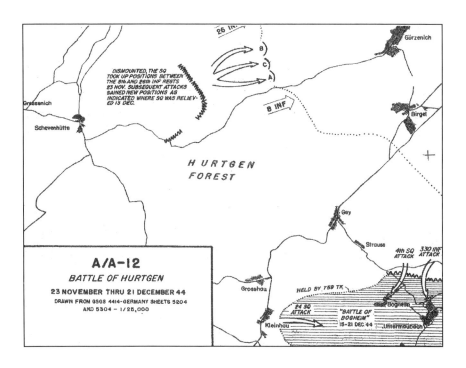

Waiting for D-Day

I entered the army at mid-autumn 1942, as did the
other recruits who joined Troop A of the 4th Cavalry
Reconnaissance Squadron. So, until landing on a French
beach on D-Day, June 6, 1944, we spent a good 20 months
waiting for D-Day. Of course we were kept busy training for
three winter months, freezing in the Black Hills of South
Dakota, expecting to fight in Norway. Then we spent six
months in California's burning Mojave Desert and two more
month in East Texas, almost as hot, expecting to battle
in North Africa. Then we had a two-week furlough to say
goodbye to our families before crossing the North Atlantic
in late November 1943, expecting to invade Europe the next
spring on some unknown D-Day.

But I hasten to add that we all enjoyed southern England,
doing road reconnaissance in a mild winter.

When not camping out on the road, we lived in Quonset
huts underneath the stands at Goodwood Park, a racing
course. A Quonset hut is a half-cylinder of corrugated
sheet metal, 10 feet high and long enough to sleep a
cavalry platoon, 30 men. You have to imagine a college
locker room with two rows of double bunk beds instead of
showers (which were outside, with the latrines). A radio and
gambling with cards or dice were also inside.

Now multiply that Quonset hut by 100,000 similar huts all
over the British Isles, and you have an idea of what it meant
to wait for D-Day. When D-Day came, there was a huge
sigh of relief. We all preferred to risk everything than spend
another day in a Quonset hut.

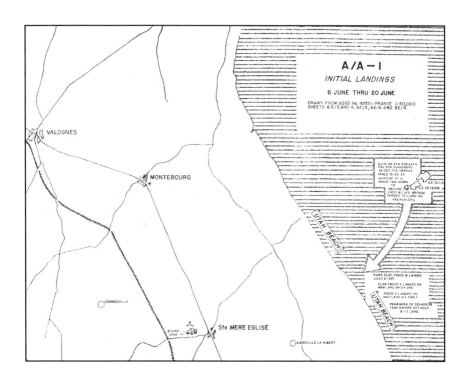

A/A—1

INITIAL LANDINGS

6 JUNE THRU 20 JUNE

DRAWN FROM GSGS No. 4250 - FRANCE 1/50,000
SHEETS 6 E/3 AND 4, 6E/5, 6E/6 AND 5E/4.

VALOGNES

MONTEBOURG

ELMS OF 4TH AND 24TH
CAV RCN SQUADRONS
SEIZED THE HEAVILY
MINED ISLES ST.
MARCOUF AT H
MINUS TWO HOURS
TO
BECOME THE
FIRST ALLIED GROUND
FORCES TO LAND ON
FRENCH SOIL

ILE DE LA
ILE DU LA TERRE

UTAH BEACH

THIRD PLAT, TROOP B LANDED
U X30 D-DAY.

ELMS TROOP A LANDED ON
MAINLAND ON D+ ONE.

TROOP E LANDED ON
MAINLAND D + TWO.

REMAINDER OF SQUADRON
CAME ASHORE BETWEEN
8-17 JUNE

GOURBESVILLE

6 JUNE
1944

Ste MERE EGLISE

AUDOUVILLE LA HUBERT

UTAH BEACH

WAR STORY 2: SAILING AGAINST ENGLAND

HOW DID I KNOW German well enough to translate for Troop A of the 4th Cavalry Recon Squadron? (A cavalry squadron consists of three line troops and a HQ troop.) With immigrant parents and relatives speaking Yiddish, a German dialect, why not?

Add to that, two years of German taught by a German immigrant, Mr. Karcher, at Chicago's John Marshall High School. And, anticipating a probable need, add to that 30 months of cramming between Pearl Harbor and D-Day.

And to that, add discussions in German over an 18-month period with Sgt. John Onken, a German immigrant who had arrived as a boy shortly after World War I. Although friendship between a private and a non-commissioned officer was taboo, a weekly conversation on the sly was OK with John, because he wanted to speak German to hear his own voice.

Finally, in England, before the invasion of Normandy, there were more than six months of late evenings listening to German radio broadcasts. These were mostly news broadcasts alternating with martial music, usually, a male chorus singing the latest hits of the Wehrmacht.

One of these hits will turn up later in this story, so I better tell you about it. *"Wir Fahren Gegend Engeland!"* (We are sailing against England!) was by far the most popular song. It implies, We Are Invading England!

By 1944, the invasion threat was over, but the tune was really catchy and retained its popularity. It wasn't long before I knew all the words and could sing along, causing some laughter in our Quonset hut if I didn't overdo it.

Our camp was underneath the stands at the Goodwood Park

race tracks, north of Chichester on the southern coast of Sussex. Walking eight miles both ways to get some beer was also a way to break the monotony. But we did actually meet the natives. Beside the bars, there was also a movie and, once before D-Day, a dance. And I have fond memories of fish and chips.

Well, the much-promised D-Day arrived, and we sailed against Germany. B Troop landed on Utah Beach shortly after H-Hour, 6:00 a.m. But two hours before that, A Troop and C Troop landed on opposite sides of Ile St. Marcouf, a small, fortified island sitting about six kilometers off Utah Beach. Taken over by the Germans after the French collapse, the fort's naval guns could have been a serious threat to the invasion. Intelligence said that the fort was not manned, but it still had to be secured in case the intelligence was not really intelligent.

My sergeant, Harvey Olson, and my corporal, Thomas Killoran, were the first U.S. soldiers to land on a French beach, rowing ashore in darkness on an inflated raft with only a flashlight to guide the landing craft. No, the fort was not manned, but the island was mined, and each troop lost one dead and several wounded due to the land mines.

A Troop lost Sgt. John Onken, the first American to die on a French beach. Needless to say, my loss was deeply felt, but all of A Troop mourned the loss. We all thought that John Onken was the best soldier in A Troop. If he could die that easily, what chance did the rest of us have?

We spent the day huddled near the shore, watching the parade of landing craft heading toward the beaches and regretting the lack of cameras to record the scene. We were too far to see the beaches, but the sounds and flashes from shore and naval gunfire were vivid enough.

Eventually, we were picked up and moved to a thoroughly secured Utah Beach. We had no vehicles and only rifles and hand grenades as arms. (If the fort had been manned by the enemy, fully equipped infantry would have landed to make an assault.) Not equipped for combat, our first mission was to guard VII Corp HQ. So, we pulled a lot of KP, messenger and guard duty.

About D+10, our vehicles, arms and equipment arrived from England, and our war really began. From Utah Beach, over the next few weeks, the VII Corps cut across the peninsula, trapping German troops too close to Cherbourg to escape. Our goal was to liberate Cherbourg, so we were pushing the enemy toward the end of the peninsula. Most of our action was dismounted, like infantry, and costly.

Eventually, about D+40, A Troop had an attack sector from the resort beaches along the Atlantic coast to about a kilometer inland. Cut off from supplies, running out of food and ammunition, the Germans started to surrender. First came an individual or two, maybe deserters, waving a white handkerchief. My interrogation was brief. They really had no information of value other than how short they were of food and ammo. The news kept getting better for us and worse for them.

Over somewhat hilly ground, we began to move more rapidly as they fell back. Then, on a beautiful, late July morning, the Krauts came out of the hills by the dozens, scruffy, without arms or helmets, waving something white. We watched in amazement as about 100 of them settled down silently, timidly, in a pasture, waiting for us to make our wishes known. Most of them had a bundle of some sort, maybe a change of underwear. Our silence and theirs was eerie. What a way for them to end a five-year struggle!

Of course, Capt. Fox was the first to react. "Sussman, can you organize this mob? We have to get them to the collection point and move on."

"Yes, sir!" In fact, I had not the slightest idea about mob

organization. By oversight, my German did not include a manual of military commands. If they had been GIs, I would have shouted: "Fall in!" and ranks would have quickly been formed. But would "*Hereinfallen!*" do the job? No idea! Instead of forming ranks, I could provoke wonderment and appear ineffective.

Because of what the Germans resembled, it occurred to me to think of them as a crowd in a railway station waiting for a train. If I were a conductor, I would shout: "Allaboooooooard!" Would that get them moving? With Capt. Fox curiously waiting for me to make my move, I was desperate enough to yell my loudest: "*Eiiinsteiiiiiigeeeeeend*!!" (Climb in!) That was the traditional conductor's call.

Immediately, about 100 scruffy German prisoners rose from the ground and started walking toward me. Captain Fox was duly impressed, but now what? I had not the faintest idea.

As they approached us within about 10 yards, standing there, one of the mob, smiling at me, shouted: "*Wo gehen wir*?" (Where are we going?) Close up and with informal attitude, his simple question, certainly apropos, gave me the impression that, yes, these were human beings, pretty much like us, wanting to know their fate.

Without really thinking about it, I had the normal human reflex to respond and to say something humorous. I could think of no other response but the name of that popular song played repeatedly on German broadcasts. So, playing for time, I yelled back: "*Wir fahren gegen Engeland*!" (We are sailing against England!)

The result was astounding! Suddenly, about 100 German prisoners doubled up in laughter! They could not control themselves, or at least gave that impression. One of them shouted: "*Endlich!*" (Finally!), Capt. Fox looked at me in wonder. He understood that I knew German but, good enough to be a stand-up comedian, with a crowd in convulsion? That was unexpected. Somehow, by accident, I had gained the captain's respect. But now what? I still had no manual of commands.

The look on the captain's face reminded me how armies move. I simply shouted out: *"Deutsche Offiziere! Stellen Sie sich bitte vor!"* (German officers, present yourselves, please!)

Several prisoners replied at once: *"Da sind keine."* (There aren't any.) Apparently, the officers, who usually spoke French, had other plans for surrendering, probably to our rear echelon troops, to soldiers less motivated by combat experience.

So, the next-best thing, non-commissioned officers: *"Deutsche Unteroffiziere! Stellen Sie sich bitte vor!"* Sure enough, a few of them approached. Asking them who was in command, one of them stepped forward and saluted. I returned the salute. My fatigues had no insignia but my high German probably gave him the impression that I was an officer. So, I saluted as a fake lieutenant. He gave his rank: F*eldwebel,* equivalent to our staff sergeant. I did not catch his name. We had now established a diplomatic relationship. The war could proceed.

There was no need for interrogation. All the information was in their faces. I explained to Feldwebel X that we had to proceed to a POW collection point about a kilometer to the rear, that his men were still in danger from the French underground seeking revenge, and that we would protect them. I didn't know how much danger there really was, but a little fear would inspire cooperation.

Feldwebel X had only one question: *"Sind Sie Deutcher?"* (Are you German?)

I replied: *"Nein, danke. Jude."* (No, thanks. Jew.)

He seemed to have an urge to say something but it passed. Without a word, he turned about and shouted the appropriate commands. Four ranks were quickly formed. After instilling the necessary amount of fear in his men, we could move out. With six of us armed – three in front, three behind – the column of four set off "at ease" for the trip to the POW collection point.

No incident before arrival, but for a half hour I walked with the largest group of the enemy I had seen. Looking at their faces, my first and lasting thought was that they were like us in every respect: tired, dirty and worried about the future. They bantered while walking, just like us! Since German ancestry is common in the U.S., their faces were very familiar. I had the urge to engage them in conversation, to get to know the enemy. It was so easy to forget that we were killing each other an hour before and now we were suddenly at peace. It was almost embarrassing to feel my change in attitude.

While I was looking at them, they were looking at me, probably wondering if I were also German. They were somehow still under the spell of my joke about invading England. Some months later, in much worse circumstances, I came to understand the laughter I had released.

When a soldier surrenders to the enemy, he undergoes a personal crisis. He is, in effect, delivering his life to a very hostile stranger. The new possessor of his fate has an unknown attitude and intention toward his prisoner. He may want revenge for the very recent death of a friend, perhaps a death under circumstance that were cruel and possibly illegal. At best, he has probably been under fire and developed a hatred. For the prisoner, everything hinges upon the mood of the captor at the moment of surrender.

When I called out as a train conductor, it was for the new prisoners a humorous tone and a sign of a good mood. They probably felt an immediate rush of hope. And my joke about invading England clinched the deal: there would be no retribution that morning. The released laughter came from their guts. My understanding of the release came from a different kind of experience. But that's another story.

Just before arriving at the collection point, Feldwebel X halted the column and brought his men to attention before moving ahead. It made everything easier at the POW collection point. We were received by a sergeant who admired the discipline. The Feldwebel saluted me once more, smiling again. As a fake lieutenant, I returned the salute. We looked at each other for a few seconds. I had an urge to say something, but it passed.

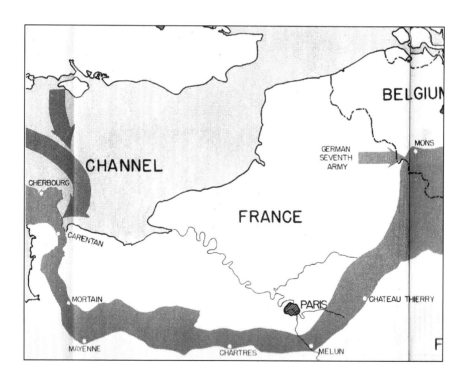

Military Cemeteries

To prepare for war, a nation needs a number of citizens who will offer their lives to save the nation. To guarantee that number, the nation's culture must venerate those who die in combat. No matter how they died, they are viewed as heroes, almost saints. Their bodies are treated with honors: a military funeral, a beautiful gravesite, a sturdy memorial with the name and rank and date of death. Assured of veneration in the worst case, we hope that a nation's youth will offer their lives in service.

It has it always been so. The climax of Homer's *Iliad* is exactly about the desecration of the body of the Trojan prince, killed by Achilles, who takes the body to his tent for further desecration. The *Iliad*'s climax comes when the King of Troy comes to the tent to beg for his son's body. His tears move Achilles to repent, and both men embrace in tears. So what may well be our greatest work of literature is all about respect for a fallen warrior. Sgt. Edward Enger (in the next story), whether he knew it or not, was just following a very long tradition.

During World War I, the enemy was buried for sanitary reasons, without ceremony. In World War II, we often passed by the bodies of fallen Germans who had to be left by a retreating army. We moved too quickly to see what happened to our own dead. In effect, we, who saw our share of dead on both sides, saw no burials in Europe.

WAR STORY 3: A BRIDGE TOO FAR

THE ONLY GOOD REASON to tell an unpleasant war story is that it illustrates something important. That's the reason I tell this unpleasant war story.

Late in July 1944, the VII Army Corps broke out of Normandy. No longer impeded by the easily defended hedgerows, our armored divisions could drive rapidly toward Germany. Eventually, in the last week of August, when resistance became disorganized, the cavalry was summoned to lead the way to Germany.

For a month we had been following the infantry, screening their flanks, picking up German stragglers. Now, after making a wide circle east and north of Paris, approaching Chateau Thierry on the Marne River, we were finally ordered to go ahead of the armor and infantry and seize an important bridge as soon as possible. My squad, augmented by two sergeants, was given the job. Racing against the sun, we were trying to get across the Marne before nightfall.

When we reached that point of no resistance and open roads, we began our road reconnaissance. That consisted first of sighting carefully for an enemy ambush at the next road bend. The squad's two jeeps would leapfrog, one of the jeeps racing to the next road bend while the other jeep, and our only armored car, were aiming at the possible ambush.

Each of the jeeps had a 30-caliber machine gun mounted on the hood to the right of the driver. The driver and gunner could peer over a cast-iron shield mounted on the hood. A 50-caliber machine gun was mounted on a post in the rear of the jeep. The M7 armored car had a 37mm cannon that could fire rounds of white phosphorous. It also had a 30-caliber machine gun to the driver's right and a 50-caliber machine gun mounted on a post in the turret. A three-second burst from all guns would deliver over 100 bullets and maybe two rounds of phosphorous.

For half of the road bends that my squad scouted, I sat to the right of the jeep driver as he was shifting into second gear and picking up speed on the way to the far road bend where a possible ambush was lurking, my hands on the 30-caliber machine gun. Was I afraid? Yes, but confident that we had had a good look and resigned to whatever happened. The dominant emotion was excitement. With the wind in my face, there was a sense of power, even euphoria, like running with a football for a touchdown that looked sure. The simple fact is that war is the most fun a young man can have, except for that part where people get hurt.

We learned real fear in the Hurtgen Forest, in the Bulge, gradually, after too many close calls, as friends disappeared while we survived.

When we got to Chateau Thierry, August 28, four days after Paris was liberated, the mood in town was delirious. The Germans had left the city south of the bridge the day before, but they could still be defending the north shore. Our squad was the first Allied troops the people had seen. Liberation was all new for them, but old for us. During August, we could experience two or three liberations in one day! For the French, after four years of military occupation, rationing, Allied bombings, arrests, executions, liberation was a big deal! Happiness reigned in the streets.

And that was our problem. With the sun setting, we were in a hurry to get to that bridge and grab it. Saving time meant saving lives. We honked but the crowd wouldn't scatter. I had to walk in front, clearing the way. Finally, the crowd thinned, and we could get into second gear. In a few minutes the river and the bridge were in view.

We parked the vehicles out of sight and walked cautiously to where we could observe the bridgehead on the other side of the river. As the summer days were getting shorter, the light was no longer good. Our field glasses found nothing, but that was not reassuring.

The bridge had two auto lanes. The river was wide, over 100 meters. If there were Germans on the far shore, they were well hidden, possibly in any of the buildings. Too many possible targets to test. There was no way we could take the bridge unless it was unguarded. If it was guarded, they had at least a squad with a machine gun. We needed a platoon to attack a squad. Almost certainly, they would have a platoon of three squads with an officer in command.

On the other hand, if it was unguarded, we could defend it while waiting for the rest of A Troop. Sgt. Edward Enger, from Blue Earth, Minnesota, had an order to take the bridge if possible. It didn't take long for him to decide. We would go!

Sgt. Enger laid out the plan. As backup, the M7 armored car, with Sgt. Richard McDermond (Mac) and three men, was set where its cannon could point at the far bridgehead and its two machine guns could cover the shore on each side of the bridge.

Two jeeps, one following the other, would cross the bridge to the other side, and the armored car would join us if all was clear. The plan was to race across, making a difficult target. The first jeep's guns would cover the bridgehead and the shore to its left. The second jeep's guns would cover the shore to the right. At the first shot from the enemy, the gunners would return fire. The drivers would continue forward for a few seconds to allow the jeeps' four machine guns to spray the source of fire. Then they would slam on the brakes and skid the jeeps into the reverse direction and race back.

The hood-mounted 30-caliber guns would have to cease fire and the 50-caliber gunners would swing around, facing the rear, and keep firing, all the way back. If we discovered the enemy only after reaching the far shore, we would either shoot our way in or shoot our way out, depending on what we found.

Robert Novak, from the South Side of Chicago, was driving the first jeep. Sgt. Enger, at his right, manned the 30-caliber machine gun. Robert Whalen, from Covington, Kentucky, manned the 50-caliber machine gun.

In the second jeep, the driver was John Klokowski, also from Chicago's South Side. From Chicago's West Side, I was at his right, on the 30-caliber machine gun. Oscar Howell, from Greensboro, North Carolina, was standing up in the back, manning the 50-caliber machine gun.

Far back from the bridge, Novak took off and John "Klok" followed a few seconds later. Novak moved into second gear before reaching the bridge, picked up speed, and was about half of the way across when a machine gun opened fire from the other side. My jeep was about one-third of the way across. We saw the muzzle flash and tracers coming from slightly to the left of the bridgehead and well beyond the shoreline. All of our guns fired at once. I could hear the M7's cannon fire and saw a white cloud near the enemy position.

After a few seconds, both jeeps skidded into the reverse direction. I had to stop firing and started to sit on the hood to leave room for Oscar to turn the 50-caliber around. At that moment, I saw Whalen without his helmet, standing in the back of the first jeep and falling out of the jeep, to his right, onto the bridge.

After the first jeep reversed direction, Novak drove it to where Whalen was lying on his back. After Klok had reversed our jeep, I was sitting on the hood, holding on to the 30-caliber gun for support, facing the rear. I could see Enger examining Whalen.

Oscar kept firing the 50 over my head, the only mobile weapon still active. The armored car was also firing all its guns. There appeared to be no more firing from the enemy. As I watched, Novak began to follow us back. When we got back to safety, Whalen was alone, lying on the bridge.

Parked behind a building, Enger explained that Bobby had at least one terrible head wound and at least two wounds in the chest. He was motionless and was not bleeding. His heart had stopped. Robert Whalen was dead.

We stood around in silence. I was the only one not smoking. After a few minutes, Enger wrote a message to Troop A HQ for me to encode and tap out. The message said only that Whalen was killed in a failed attempt to seize the bridge and gave our location but nothing else.

Waiting for a reply, Enger broke the silence: "I should have taken Bobby with us."

We assured him that he had made the right choice. A few seconds could have cost more lives. We would get Whalen's body in any case.

I copied the reply to my message as it beeped in: Troop A HQ would inform us when they had set up a bivouac just before the city. With no more to do until morning, we were about to open C-ration cans when a few civilians approached. One of them was a school teacher I had questioned earlier.

The teacher invited us to a banquet in a close-by community hall. Food and drinks were laid out on tables. Liberation was being celebrated. Champagne was flowing, and there were trays with slices of bread smeared with all kinds of stuff. It was what GIs called "horses' doovers." The atmosphere was French conversation and laughter. On a radio, someone in Paris was describing the celebrations.

When the teacher revealed that I spoke a decent French, some very happy people asked all the questions that I had been asked during each liberation. I barely responded, managing to keep my mouth full to avoid talking. I did not mention losing Whalen. Why throw cold water on their celebration?

I left Novak, Klok and Howell with a crowd practicing their English and joined the two sergeants eating and drinking, surrounded by another crowd practicing their English. Gradually, we were eating less and drinking more.

The champagne was doing its work in what was becoming a wake in the midst of a celebration. Between sips of champagne, Enger repeated that he should have taken Bobby off the bridge. Finally, Mac, tired of hearing that, said: "Let's go get Bobby and bring him back."

Enger's face lit up. "Yes! Let's go!"

This was crazy, contrary to the rules as well as to good sense. It could end badly. No matter. Somehow, it seemed to be the right thing to do. Maybe it was the champagne. OK, it was the champagne. We went out to our vehicles, which were being guarded by the M7 armored car crew, Robert Schaeffer, Irving Mendell and Manuel Mendez. The radio had informed them that Troop A HQ had set up a bivouac just before the city. Sgt. Enger drove there and brought back our medic, Geiger, and a stretcher.

Four of us, the two sergeants, Geiger and myself, went in one jeep back toward the bridge, flying the Red Cross flag. There was now only moonlight. We parked the jeep far from the bridgehead. Geiger, with his Red Cross helmet and carrying the flag, led the way to the body. If there were Germans still on guard, they respected the flag.

We lifted Bobby onto the stretcher and carried him back to the jeep. While Mac and I walked all the way back to the community hall, Enger and Geiger drove back to the HQ bivouac. Enger left

Bobby with Geiger at his first aid tent and rejoined us at the community hall.

Taking turns at guard, we continued the wake with more horses' doovers and champagne. When we had mourned enough and returned to the bivouac, it was well after midnight.

So, who was Robert Whalen? Bobby was an Appalachian, one generation removed from Appalachia, with all the implications. Yes, he was a racist. And a homophobe. And a misogynist. And an anti-Semite. And probably more. In other words, he was, at that time, a typical American, like a hundred million others! And he was also our brother-in-arms, pulling his weight, sharing our fate. If you could see Robert Whalen as I saw him just before his death, standing in the jeep, rushing toward the enemy, the wind in his face, a weapon in his hands spitting fire at the enemy, you would see what I saw – an American hero!

And we could not leave him on the bridge where, at dawn, the crows would peck at his body. Ed Enger had to go and get him and carry him back for a proper burial, damn the consequences!

What was motivating Sgt. Enger, you may ask. I did, too. He seemed to be obsessed. Of course, I can only guess, but my best guess is that Ed Enger sensed a responsibility for the death of Robert Whalen. He had taken a chance with unknown odds and had guessed wrong. And Bobby's death was the result.

Such decisions are made in combat as often as leaves fall in autumn. Every commander has such a burden but some cases are different than others. It was probably easier for Gen. Eisenhower to send a million men into danger on D-Day than for Sgt. Enger to risk one squad for a bridge. Different stakes, different bets to be made, and different attitudes on losing the bet. That's why soldiers quickly recognize and look up to good leaders like Ed Enger, and are willing to follow them through the gates of hell.

Eventually, Robert Whalen was buried at the American cemetery in Epinal, France, east of Paris, in the Lorraine region.

Of the ten members of the squad that day, only six went home. Of the three men in my Jeep, I was the only one that went home.

Oscar Howell and John Klokowski were killed in action later and buried in an American cemetery in Europe. Manuel Mendez was killed in action later and was returned to his family in Detroit, Michigan.

May they all rest in peace.

WAR STORY 4: A SNIPER'S VIEW

WHY WAS I ABLE to translate the French language for Troop A of the 4th Cavalry Reconnaissance Squadron? Because in England, several months before D-Day, Sgt. McDermond ordered me and a few other A-troopers to learn French. Our aptitude scores were high enough to bet that we could learn a useful amount of French.

I was given a small piece of luggage that opened to reveal a portable phonograph record player, headphones and a crank handle for winding up the 78-rpm motor. There was also a box of 15 records, each side containing one lesson delivered by voices of professors at the Sorbonne University of Paris. Three books included the texts of 30 lessons, a grammar and a dictionary.

Frankly, I fell in love with the French language. If I could make sounds like that, *mademoiselles* would swoon! The schedule provided for two hours of study in the morning and two hours in the afternoon, to which I added two more evening hours. I almost finished the course.

Unfortunately, sometime after D-Day, on meeting my first Frenchman, I was dismayed to find that he was not a Sorbonne professor and that his rapid, colloquial French was Greek to me! Nevertheless, my French was good enough to ask a farmer how recently he had seen any Germans. And also good enough to ask the farmer for *calvados*, the local apple brandy, in a trade for cigarettes. The quality of their brandy was about the same as American applejack. They kept the good, 30-year-old stuff hidden, but applejack was good enough for my sergeant, Harvey Olson, who regarded calvados as a necessity, unfortunately not provided by the U.S. army.

One of the first combat duties of the squadron was protecting the left flank of the 4th Infantry Division as it advanced from

Utah Beach to the other side of the peninsula. We looked for trouble by poking around, starting sometimes at dawn. Sgt. Olson would typically form a foot patrol by pointing to individuals in the platoon while saying, "You, you and you. And you too, Sussman." So, it was not the Lord, but Sussman, who, with his French vocabulary, would provide Olson with calvados. Whatever else happened on a patrol, we usually came back with a half-filled wine bottle.

As much as I would rather avoid a dawn patrol, I really did like talking to Norman farmers while Olson was sipping a small glass. Rarely, as we crossed Normandy, did I manage to meet mademoiselles, who were probably kept hidden along with the 30-year-old calvados. And the few that I did meet never swooned.

One sunny morning, about half-way across the Normandy peninsula, where the hilly land was near its highest altitude, we did find trouble. The date was about D+20, the end of June 1944. We, a four-man patrol led by Sgt. Olson, were walking westward through fallow meadows. With a million or more French prisoners of war working in Germany, only the best land was farmed.

 We were climbing up a steep hill with a wide, bushy crest. As we approached the crest of the hill, we spread out from left to right, crawling through the bushes to examine the landscape ahead of us. The first peek revealed an amazing sight.

Ahead, the hill descended into an open field, a meadow fit for grazing. But, instead of cows, we saw, about 300 meters from us, more than 50 German soldiers advancing toward us at a slow walk! Spread out in one row, from left to right, about five meters apart, they carried rifles across their chests, ready to be used. In the center of the line and about 10 meters in front of it, a commanding officer set the pace. What remained of a German infantry company was moving toward us, intending to climb up into our laps! Very soon, we would have to move!

To explain that sight, I have to say something about tactics. When American infantry moves down a roadway, it proceeds in two columns, one on each side of the road with lots of space between men to minimize casualties. Our air superiority eliminated the danger of strafing.

German infantry would do the same at night, but during daylight that was not safe. If a Spitfire were to dive out of the clouds and strafe their column on a roadway, they would be hemmed in by roadside hedgerows, unable to escape bullets or napalm. So during the day they preferred to travel in open fields where they could scramble in any direction. By walking abreast, they were all a similar distance from any target before them and could concentrate their fire without hitting a friend.

They had much more fire power than we had, but we did have one advantage: the sun was overhead, behind us. To see us, hidden in the brush, they would have had to look directly into the sun. They could only guess at the source of our rifle fire. Of course, I saw no reason to fire. We were scouting for information, not to win the war!

The captain was headed straight out of the Normandy peninsula. Maybe he thought they could go all the way to Germany, but more likely he expected to end up in a POW camp, where they could finally get a meal.

It was fascinating to watch them getting nearer, but time was working against us. None of us spoke until the captain was less than 200 meters away. Then, almost at once, three of us whispered: "Oley, we have to get out of here!"

Olson was silent for a few seconds. Then he said: "Yes, but first I want to get that captain! Aim at his chest but don't fire until you hear my shot!"

What an idea: an execution! All of us had sharpshooter medals, and all except me had been hunting since the age of 10. We were right at the hillcrest in a prone position, rifles poised to fire, and could drop back below the hillcrest to safety in a few seconds after firing. We had to run back with a report in any case. Why not?

As the captain started up the hill, it became obvious to us that Olson was going to wait until we could see the whites of his eyes!

We had time to think. Maybe too much time.

Before this day, I had fired at enemy soldiers at a distance but they were moving rapidly so there was no time to aim carefully. We got off as many shots as possible, but the targets would drop out of sight when fired upon. We seldom knew how effective our shots were.

So there I was, for the first time, really aiming carefully at a human being, a certain kill. He appeared to be around 30, wore glasses, and was athletic enough to start up the hill without breaking stride. He probably graduated from a university. He could easily be married, maybe with children. He could be thinking of them. Yet, within one minute, he would be dead.

And I had other thoughts. When I was about 10 years old, 1933, I saw a marvelous movie, *All Quiet on the Western Front*. It was based upon a book describing the grim life of a German infantry soldier during several years of World War I. The author was wounded five times, so we know that the description is accurate. In the novel, the soldier, Paul Boemer, survived many artillery bombardments, gas attacks and fierce hand-to-hand struggles with bayonets. In the novel's ending, very near the end of the war, on a quiet day with no combat, Paul Boemer was killed.

The book does not describe the manner of death at all, but the movie ends with the portrayal. First, we were shown a bright day over a green field. A butterfly lands on a flower near the soldier, who collected butterflies. While he reaches very slowly to capture the insect, the camera cuts to a French sniper taking aim with his telescopic sights. Then the camera shifts back to a close-up showing only the soldier's hand, moving slowly, very slowly toward the butterfly. As the hand moves, we see it suddenly jerk up. Then we see the hand drop slowly to the ground as the butterfly, the symbol of life, flies away, and we know that Paul Boemer is dead. You can see why the director got two Oscars.

Walking out of the dark B&K Central Park Theater into the bright daylight on Roosevelt Road in Chicago's West Side, my memory of that moment, as a ten-year-old, is how much I hated that French sniper. Yes, the French were our ally and the Germans our enemy, but by the end of the movie, audience sympathy was with the German soldier, who only wanted to survive and go home. And the war was almost over!

As the German officer climbed the hill, I remembered that French sniper. I was now that hated sniper.

I was conflicted. If an enemy is charging toward you or shooting at you, you will fire at the enemy with a sense of fear or even panic. Emotionally, you know why you are pulling the trigger. But as a well-hidden sniper, you have no fear or panic. A sniper fires calmly at someone who is not an immediate threat to him. In this case, the Germans were perhaps hours away from a prison camp, where they would be rendered harmless.

This captain had gone through five years of war. And the war was almost over. If he got to the POW camp, he would eventually go home to his family. He could pick up the pieces, have a career, maybe do something good. He could be a Nazi, but two-thirds of the Germans voted against Hitler in 1933. And German army officers tried to assassinate Hitler. Everybody, good or evil, gets dragged into a war. How can any individual be judged?

I must admit that I was naïve. I had read all the well-known German writers. I had great respect for German culture, at the top in science, mathematics, music and literature. This was June 1944, before the discovery of the death camps and other atrocities that the German army had watched in silence, if not participating. I looked at Germans as any other people now caught in a trap. Such naivete did not last the war, but it lasted through Normandy.

So, here I was, about to kill Paul Boemer. The only motivation for a sniper to kill is duty or hatred of the enemy or both. Did I hate this Paul Boemer enough to keep him out of a POW camp? Maybe. Maybe not.

Of course, his death was inevitable. I could easily miss him, and no one would know but my conscience would be clear.

On one hand, if I killed him, it would be in cold blood. There is something in human nature that instinctively resists killing a fellow human being in cold blood. I would be killing him like Cain killed Abel. Did I waste my time reading Kant and Niebuhr?

On the other hand, a German officer could not surrender unless he ran out of ammunition, and that was not the case, so there was no way that Paul Boemer could be thought of as anything but a deadly enemy. In any case, I had been given an order, and I had a duty to obey.

So, where does that leave the philosophers? They knew nothing about the logic of war. No more than a 10-year-old! So I had to overcome instinct and aim well.

The officer kept a steady pace uphill. I kept my sights on Paul Boemer's chest, following his movements. Olson waited until the captain was about 30 meters away, home plate to second base, slowing his pace as the hill became steeper. Olson's shot rang right into my ear. As I was squeezing the trigger, Paul Boemer moved away, reacting to the hit, and stopped only on the ground. Then, within a couple of seconds, four more of our shots went off, and we scrambled back to safety behind and below the hill crest.

Olson shouted "Grenades!" as he pulled a pin and heaved one over the crest, as far as he could. We all did the same as a flurry of bullets cracked the air well over our heads. Then we ran down the hill, trying to keep our balance. Back on the flat ground, we kept running until the hill was out of sight.

That was my first well-aimed shot at a human being and also the last shot before which I had time to think about the inner life of my target. Just so you know, that's the worst way to shoot someone.

That evening I could not stop thinking about Harvey Olson. Off duty, in a bar, Olson was usually rowdy and only too happy to get into a fight. I was afraid he could get us into trouble. But, while I had been amazed by the sight of the advancing enemy, thinking about the captain's life and my duties as his enemy, Harvey Olson had only one thought: how to inflict the maximum damage upon the enemy at a minimum risk to his men. I was acting like a philosopher, and Harvey Olson was a soldier, a commander capable of meeting his responsibilities.

He had seen the enemy, planned an ambush, and carried it off with astounding success. He had killed the leader and maybe a few more, had probably wounded a dozen of the enemy, and had forced as many as two dozen more to help the wounded. He had effectively disabled the enemy with a minimum of ammunition and no friendly losses.

It was a lesson for me. I was naive. I would have to learn soldiering and learn fast. Fortunately, I had a great teacher. Harvey Olson won several medals, survived the war, stayed in the army, fought in Korea, won more medals, went home, and passed away peacefully at the age of 82. You can google him for more information.

Whatever my thoughts were that evening, "Oley" had only one regret: that the patrol had returned without a bottle of calvados. Sgt. Harvey Olson was absolutely right: calvados *was* a necessity, unfortunately not provided by the U.S. Army.

Unit Citation

Just before the "Battle of the Bulge" the 106th Infantry Division, fresh from the United States with minimal training, was thinly deployed over a wide front near the Belgium-German border. Almost all of its men were killed, wounded or captured after a surprise attack by an overwhelming German force. The battle described below occurred because of, during, and near that tragedy.

* * * * * * * * * * * * * *

HEADQUARTERS SEVENTH ARMY
TESTAMENTARY ABSTRACT
APO 768   US ARMY
GENERAL ORDERS}   28 August 1945
                    }
NUMBER   450 }

E X T R A C T

Battle Honors – Citation of Unit
By direction of the President, under provisions of Section IV, Circular No. 333, War Department, 1943, the following named organization is cited for outstanding performance of duty in action.

The 4th CAVALRY RECONNAISANCE SQUADRON, MECHANIZED, is cited for conspicuously distinguishing itself in battle against the enemy on 21 and 22 December 1944. The squadrons mission was to attack in its zone and secure Bogheim, Germany, and the high ground to the southeast of the town. Previous actions in the Hurtgen Forest had reduced the troops to between 55 and 70 men each. Nevertheless, two battle groups of the 942nd German Infantry Regiment, 353rd Infantry Division, and one company of the 6th Parachute Regiment, which then represented one of the finest fighting units of the German Army, were completely destroyed during the course of this action. On the morning of 21 December 1944, in dense fog and under heavy concentrations of enemy artillery, the squadron forced an entry into Bogheim. Resistance was fanatical, necessitating tortuous house-to-house fighting. By 1400 hours all resistance in the town had ceased but the Troop Commanders of all troops directly committed had either been killed or seriously wounded and five of the nine platoon leaders of the Reconnaisance Troops evacuated. Twenty five percent of the enlisted personnel had also become casualties. Again, on the morning of the following day, still under heavy artillery saturation, at times reaching a density of two hundred rounds per hour, the remainder of the Squadron drove and fought its way to the top of the ridge to the southeast, held by vastly superior enemy forces in excellent defenses. Almost completely exhausted from the heavy sustained fighting of the previous day, the troops nevertheless attacked at a dead run over two hundred yards of open ground uphill to the ridge. Only the gallantry and esprit de corps of the officers and men above and beyond the call of duty enabled the Squadron to reorganize again and again after losing many Troop Commanders, Platoon Leaders, and other key personnel vital to the continued functioning of a tactical unit. The gallantry and supreme devotion to duty of the officers and men of this Squadron and the magnificence of their performance were in keeping with the highest traditions of the United States Cavalry and the United States Armed Forces.

BY COMMAND OF LIEUTENANT GENERAL KEYES:
                                                      PEARSON MENCHER
                                                      Brigadier General GSC
                                                      Chief of Staff

OFFICIAL: S/   W. G. Caldwell
                    Colonel AGD
                    Adjutant General
A TRUE EXTRACT COPY:
                         (Signed) LYLE B.F.HAYTER
                                        1st Lt., Cavalry
                                        Asst. Adjutant

EPILOGUE

DURING 20 MONTHS OF TRAINING and 11 months of combat, A-Troopers changed from being strangers, to being companions who shared bread, to being friends who shared burdens, to being brothers who shared life and death. And it is that brotherhood that explains the ability of soldiers to do their duty as they face death every day.

A Presidential Unit Citation (see p. 42) was presented to the entire 4th Cavalry Squadron for its performance during the Battle of the Bulge when our paratroopers were being surrounded at Bastogne. On the way to rescue the paratroopers, the Germans had fortified a ridge with artillery that could delay the rescue. The squadron was tasked with removing that artillery, whatever the cost. They succeeded in removing that artillery, but at a great cost.

The citation uses the words "gallantry" and "supreme devotion to duty" for that quality which we all know more simply as "courage." That quality springs not only from patriotism but also from what the citation calls "esprit de corps," which is French for "team spirit" – but I know it as "brotherhood," which, more than anything else, explains the source of the courage displayed.

If you can imagine yourself among your brothers when the "Go!" command is called, all your brothers on your right and on your left will go, and you will go with them because it is your duty to go, but also because, in the past weeks and months, at the risk of their own lives, they saved yours – more than once – and now they are going into danger and they will need you. And so you will go with them out of gratitude and loyalty and a brotherly love that will drive you above and beyond the call of duty.

And that brotherhood is the reason, the true reason, that when the "Go!" command is called, everyone will go, and everyone will do what must be done, whatever the cost.

When soldiers swear to obey all orders without hesitation, they make a promise they intend to keep. Keeping their promise and paying the price of freedom, 37 of my A Troop brothers, out of 140 men at full strength, were killed in action. Their names are on the next page. Unnamed here are my other A Troop brothers who also kept their promise and paid the price of freedom, suffering more than 100 wounds, far too often severe and permanent.

Now you know how those promises were kept. To give meaning and value to their sacrifice and to ensure that these honored dead shall not have died in vain, please do whatever you can to make our leaders see the use of armed force as the very last resort.

Promise Keepers:

A-TROOPERS KILLED IN ACTION DURING WORLD WAR II

Edward B Abdo, Pvt.

Kenneth E Berggren, 1st Lt.

Martin J Biringer, Pvt.

Robert L Blaha, Pvt.

Emil A Bukowski, Cpl.

William F Burgess, Pvt.

Earl F Chmela, Pfc.

Arthur Clowrey, Pvt.

Wayne Cloyd, Pvt.

John J Coyne, T/5

David Cunningham, 2nd Lt.

Wayne O. Duncan, Pvt.

Ray G Elliot, Jr, S/Sgt.

Lawrence L Elman, 2nd Lt.

George W Forbes, S/Sgt.

Ralph O Grear, T/5

Charlie T Guy, T/5

Warren L Hawks, T/5

Charlie Holleman, T/5

Robert Horlick, T/5

William B Horton, Pvt.

Oscar Howell, T/5

Lehman Kilby, Pfc.

Alvin T King, T/4

John Klokowski, Pfc.

William J Liddell, Pvt.

Jack D Lynn, Sgt.

William S McCauley, Capt.

Manuel J Mendez, Pvt.

Norbert J O'Donnell, T/5

John C Onken, Sgt.

Leonard W Richter, Pvt.

Vernon V Ryan, Cpl.

Robert J Whalen, Pvt.

Kenneth Williams, Pfc.

Phillip R Ziegler, Pvt.

Harry J Zielinski, Pfc.

Return to Civilian Life

1946-47: Roosevelt University, Chicago. This was its first year of existence, accepting Black students. Studied languages: Spanish, Italian, Russian. Economics class with Prof. Abba Lerner (google him!). English Lit with Harold Washington, as classmate and frequent lunch companion; he became Chicago's first Black mayor.

Summer 1946: Bellhop in Catskill Mountains of New York.

Summer 1947: Drove a Yellow Cab in Chicago.

1948: Dropped college for politics with Henry Wallace. Utter failure.

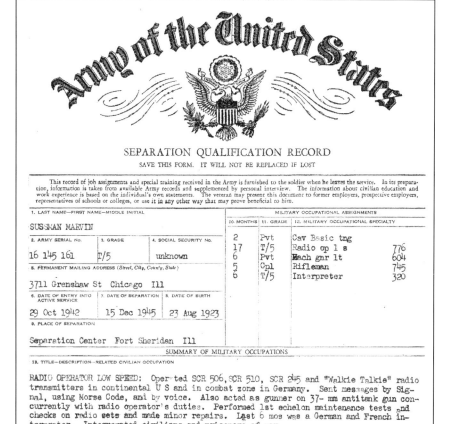

1949-1952: Illinois Institute of Technology. BS Electrical Engineering; BS Math (evenings), 1959.

1953: American Typewriter Co., Chicago. Tried to operate a mechanical typewriter from a punched tape input.

1954: Designed transformers for electronic application. Attended Spanish class evenings at Downtown Chicago YMCA, intending to quit and go to Mexico. In May, met classmate Miguelle Genty, with the same intention. From France, visiting her mother living in Chicago, she had a degree in English Lit from the Sorbonne in Paris. I quit the job in June, left with Miguelle on a Greyhound bus for Mexico. Lived in a "pension" for $1/day; lunch at Univ. of Mexico for a dime. Traveled Mexico in buses. Came back late September, broke. Got a job, a car, an apartment, a wife.

1955-1977: International Harvester, Manufacturing Research Dept. Industrial engineering; playing with computers; having kids; protesting Vietnam; meeting Tom Hayden, Dave Dellinger and other Chicago Seven defendants.

With Miguelle

1978-1987: BorgWarner Corp., Manufacturing Research Dept. Industrial engineering, still playing with computers, putting three boys through college.

1987: Miguelle's mother died, leaving a home in France.

1988-2004: We spent six months every year in Ollainville, outer suburb of Paris, 35 minutes by train.

1991: Trip to USSR by train from Paris to live in Minsk with first cousins. Returned three weeks before collapse of U.S.S.R.

2004-2014: Retired, living downtown, Elmhurst. Miguelle developed dementia.

2014-present: Retired in Park Place of Elmhurst. Studying macroeconomics, the most important subject. Writing essays, attempting to explain it to high school graduates.

2018, Sept 2: Miguelle passed after 64 years of marriage, all of them, except the last few, really great.

To the Squadron, Fall 1945

...

There is no need to praise the Fourth Cavalry: that has been done by our higher commanders. But what can we say of our experiences?

There is none among us who can put them into words, for only the greatest artists can depict such things. Who can adequately describe the icy fear or blind rage of battle, or the apprehension that precedes combat? Who will set down in words what it feels like to send a patrol on a dangerous mission, or to lead a patrol on a foggy night, or to be a member of one?

Everyone has longed for the voice of his loved ones and the sight of his home, and it is not necessary to describe the boredom of inactivity and long waiting, but what man will undertake to tell how the presence of a brave comrade at his side inspired warm confidence and courage when Death seemed about to strike? Or to tell of the meaning of comradeship in wartime? Or what are the thoughts of those whose work is behind the lines when they get the word that their friends are in desperate need of help?

Why do men fight or work for many days and nights with not enough sleep and not enough food? Can anyone give a description of that fatigue? Or of the cumulative misery of incessant chilly rain and fog and mud when a man must live in them for days?

We have seen deeds of high courage. We have watched our brothers in arms go down. We have camped in the ruins of great cities and in lovely valleys unmarked by war. We have made long night marches half asleep.

There is no poet yet to sing of deep pine forests where the enemy lay hidden, or of bitter cold and snowy open fields. We who were there have not the gift to portray in words or oils those scenes or those events. Unfaltering valor, dread and loneliness, duty, loyalty and honor are words that do not come glibly to our lips.

Many have written and will write of the mighty tyranny that was crushed, and of noble victories, but it was a long way from Normandy to the Harz Mountains, and there is no one to tell of it as it was. Each man must recall it for himself as each saw it for himself.

Between the lines of this account we shall all discover memories. The story itself means little apart from these, and is not meant to.

One memory we shall cherish above all others: the steadfastness of the men with whom we served.

EDWARD C. DUNN,
Lieutenant Colonel, 4th Cavalry.

JOHN F. RHOADES,
Lieutenant Colonel, 4th Cavalry.

67444573R00030

Made in the USA
Columbia, SC
28 July 2019